OFFICE
Feng Shui

OFFICE

Feng Shui

Creating Harmony in Your Work Space

by Darrin Zeer

Illustrations by Frank Montagna

CHRONICLE BOOKS

SAN FRANCISCO

Library of Congress Cataloging-in-Publication Data:

Zeer, Darrin.
  Office Feng Shui : creating harmony in your workspace /
by Darrin Zeer.
    p. cm.
  ISBN 0-8118-4215-0
  1. Feng shui. 2. Success in business. 3. Environmental
psychology.
I. Title.
  BF1779.F4Z44 2004

  133.3'337--dc21   2003007906

Manufactured in China

Design by **Julie Vermeer**.

Distributed in Canada by Raincoast Books
9050 Shaughnessy Street
Vancouver, British Columbia V6P 6E5

10 9 8 7 6 5 4 3 2 1

Chronicle Books LLC
85 Second Street
San Francisco, California 94105

www.chroniclebooks.com

Organized office . . .
ORGANIZED MIND!

CONTENTS

QUICK HELP GUIDE

INTRODUCTION

What if you arrived at work and it felt like home? How would that be?

Work is too often associated with negative images of stress, tension, multitasking, and tight deadlines. Since we all spend so much of our lives on the job, why not transform our offices? Imagine working in an environment that helps you relax while accomplishing plenty at the same time. *Office Feng Shui* will guide you down a path to create simple, conscious living in the workplace.

Feng shui, considered the "art of placement," is a five-thousand-year-old philosophy that originated in China. The term *feng shui* literally translates to "wind and water," symbolizing the subtle energies that flow through our environment. The mystical, creative forces of feng shui are quite simple to put into practice; they require little expense and they produce powerful results. *Office Feng Shui* offers suggestions on how to create an organized workplace that looks good, feels good, and is empowering to whomever works in it.

I've translated the ancient Chinese art of feng shui into a modern, practical guide with quick tips so that anyone can easily understand and implement them. I've also adapted feng shui maps for the desktop and the office. You will find helpful tips whether you are trying to find the best location to sit, cleaning out your files, searching for peace of mind, shuffling the stuff on your desktop, or rearranging your entire office. Experiment with some of these suggestions to see if they don't create pleasant and positive changes in your work attitude, your productivity, and your peace of mind. Try randomly flipping the book open for instant relief, or go to the Quick Help Guide on page 9 for tips on specific problems. And remember the *Office Feng Shui* mantra: To clear your mind, clear your work space.

Five Feng Shui Tips
for the Workplace

1   Take care of your office . . . it's where you spend
    a large part of each weekday.

2   For a fresh perspective, look at your work space
    through a visitor's eyes.

3   Be open to change in yourself and around you.

4   Pay attention to the details.

5   Try implementing *Office Feng Shui* ideas into
    your work space each day to enjoy more
    calmness and productivity.

FENG SHUI DEMYSTIFIED

To understand the art of feng shui, it's important to be aware of the powerful, hidden forces that surround us.

On a very subtle level, beyond our ability to see, lies an ocean of energy that ebbs and flows in and around us. The Chinese refer to this energy as *chi* (pronounced "chee"). In the world of business we need to pay attention to the chi in our workplace. A clean, organized office space with everything in order allows energy to flow and frees you up to calmly mastermind your projects.

Chapter One
FENG SHUI FOR YOUR DESK
WORK WISELY!

MESSY DESK SYNDROME

*Keeping your personal space in order opens
the flow of chi and stimulates your creativity.*

At times, all of us are affected by messy desk syndrome. Especially during busy times, paper can pile up and chaos can slowly creep in. Clutter creates stagnation, reduces your effectiveness, and leaves you feeling lethargic and confused. Don't be hard on yourself—this is normal and okay for short periods. Instead of tackling the mess all at once, you may find it helpful and therapeutic to take little organization breaks at various points during your day. Do it first thing in the morning to help you get started on the right foot. Or, try making a weekly date with you and your stuff. One week organize your contacts (Rolodex, address book, etc.), the next week your computer desktop, and so on.

*The bravest sight in the world is to see
a great man struggling against adversity.*
—Seneca

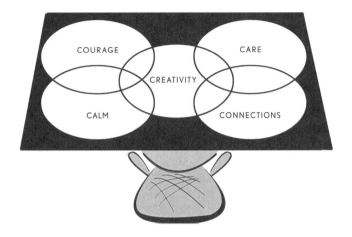

DESKTOP MAP **OF SUCCESS**

Though your desk has limited space, it is one area in the office where you can freely make feng shui enrichments.

For this book I've created a Desktop Map of Success, which is divided into five interrelated circles. The five circles are called Calm, Courage, Care, Connections, and Creativity. These are the cornerstones of a successful career. You can meditate on these areas of the desk or turn to "Desktop Celebration!" on page 20, where you will find specifics on how to enrich these areas of your work life using object placement and other feng shui practices.

Circle of Calm (bottom left of desk)

When you're calm and focused, you will succeed in all your projects.

Circle of Courage (top left of desk)

It takes courage to tackle all the work challenges that you face day after day.

Circle of Care (top right of desk)

Demonstrate care and compassion for yourself and those you work with.

Circle of Connections (bottom right of desk)

When you reach out, you can make powerful contacts with clients, coworkers, and everyone else you interact with.

Circle of Creativity (center of desk)

When all of the other desktop circles are in balance, you will have unlocked the key to unlimited creativity. Let this creative-power spot in the center of your desk be the launchpad for your success.

DESKTOP **CELEBRATION!**

Enrichments for Your Desktop.

For inspiration and support, you can implement feng shui enrichments to specific areas on your desk. Study the Desktop Map of Success on the previous two pages and incorporate some of the following suggestions. While you are working, take time to pause and focus on the five circles of success on your desk. Repeat the affirmations to maintain calm, courage, care, connections, and creativity throughout your day.

- **Circle of Calm:** *"I stay calm in all situations."*
  If you desire peace and wisdom, place a religious icon or nature postcard in this circle.

- **Circle of Courage:** *"I am courageous and willing to take risks."*
  If you desire more prosperity, place a small money tree or a fish bowl in this circle.

- **Circle of Care:** *"I am caring with myself and others."*
  If you desire more care, place a family photo or flowers in this circle.

- **Circle of Connections:** *"I stay connected with myself and others."*
  If you desire more clients and support, place a small globe of the world in this circle.

- **Circle of Creativity:** *"I have unlimited creativity."*
  If you desire more success, it is essential that you keep this power spot in perfect order.

COMPUTER **PLACEMENT**

Your computer is a source of lively, powerful chi.

Keep your computer and its screen clean, since it is most
likely your primary source of business. You may not be able
to move your computer around on your desk, but make sure
that when you're working at your computer, you face straight
toward it. Use a wrist rest to help support your wrists while
you type. Make sure that there is no glare reflecting off your
monitor. A good combination glare screen and radiation filter
can help prevent headaches and eyestrain. If you have the
freedom to move your computer around on your desk, set it up
so that your body is comfortable while you type. Feel free to
cover the screen with an attractive cloth when it's not in use.

*The best way to escape
from a problem is to solve it.
—Anonymous*

COMPUTER
CLUTTER

Just like your actual desktop, your desktop screen tends to accumulate clutter.

- All files and folders should be organized and stored in a neat manner on your screen.

- To avoid the feeling of work hanging over your head, don't let your inbox overflow with e-mails. Develop files to organize and store your e-mails.

- Create folders in which to store your shortcuts and applications.

- Choose a background screen color that soothes your eyes. Purple is an auspicious color and calming for the mind.

- Display a soothing nature screen saver. Mountain or ocean scenes will promote stability and charge your computer screen with chi.

He who asks a question is a fool for five minutes; he who does not ask a question remains a fool forever.
—*Chinese proverb*

COMMUNICATION
TRANSFORMATION

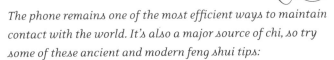

The phone remains one of the most efficient ways to maintain contact with the world. It's also a major source of chi, so try some of these ancient and modern feng shui tips:

- Place an attractive cloth (red is a prosperous color) under the phone to help activate its energy and get the phone ringing with positive opportunities.

- Keep your phone clean and shiny as a sign of devotion to your work.

- Set up your phone on the same side of the desk as your favored listening ear. This way the telephone wire won't awkwardly cross your desk or computer screen.

- Make calls in comfort by using a headset. This will greatly decrease any neck or shoulder tension and will help you painlessly multitask during calls.

- For good luck, try taping a penny or Chinese coin to the base of the phone to generate good fortune.

- Program frequently used phone numbers into your phone so you can speed-dial when you're busy.

- Display a small card with words of inspiration on the phone, as a reminder to be friendly and attentive during your conversations.

SITTING **ZEN**

While sitting for long periods of time, you may find that your posture and mood slump down in disharmony. This ancient Zen meditation posture will relieve aching muscles and lift your spirits in seconds.

1   Sit toward the front edge of your chair, away from the back support.

2   Straighten your back and tuck in your chin.

3   Your arms and shoulders should be kept as relaxed as possible. Feel your shoulders sink lower as you breathe.

4   Interlace your fingers and rest them on your belly. Feel your hands rise and fall with each breath.

5   Inhale slowly and steadily through your nose; exhale at the same rate.

6   Make no attempt to rush your breathing. Try in a relaxed manner to increase the volume and length of each breath.

7   Keep your eyes relaxed, unfocused, and (preferably) open. Feel the powerful chi flowing through your body.

Practice this technique for a few minutes between meetings and calls.

CHAIR TAI CHI

Reenergizing Rocking. This exercise will help you sharpen your focus on the work in front of you. You can try this while making calls, working on the computer, or anytime throughout the day.

1   As you sit at your desk, plant your feet firmly on the ground.

2   Sit forward, away from the back support.

3   Lift your heels up and shift your weight onto your toes, holding for a moment.

4   Rock your feet back onto your heels, raising your toes off the floor, and feel the stretch in your calves.

5   Continue rocking your feet forward and back, stretching your feet and toes.

Back Benefit. This exercise will help keep your back limber while you're sitting at your desk.

1   As you sit, straighten your spine upward.

2   Take in a deep breath and puff your chest outward.

3   As you exhale, release your chest downward and let your back slump down.

4   Repeat this motion of stretching up and then slumping down until you feel relief.

COMFORTABLE THRONE

Your chair is your throne of power and comfort.

Make sure that you find a good chair that feels cozy and
supportive. A fully covered, wide-backed chair is empower-
ing. Armrests also provide support and are essential to those
who do lots of computer work. Make sure that the armrests
keep your elbows at right angles (90 degrees) as you type. It
is uplifting for your posture and mind if your chair has good
lumbar support for your lower back. The seat height should
be adjustable to help you align yourself with the desk. If you
are not comfortable in the chair that your company provides,
bring in your favorite chair from home. Your comfort will
more than repay the effort and expense.

A leader is a dealer in hope.
—Napoléon Bonaparte

UP AGAINST **THE WALL**

Are you feeling lethargic and unable to complete your tasks? You may literally be up against the wall and need to move your desk. Where your desk is located can make the difference between success and failure.

Walls are best to back you up and can be confronting or limiting when they're right in front of you. If you have the freedom to move your desk, try to situate it in a position of support. If possible, sit facing the entrance to your office. If you sit with your back to the door you'll block chi and will feel startled each time someone enters your work space. Your body will feel tense, and your neck will get sore from constantly turning to see who is at the door. Symbolically, you may be turning your back on life's opportunities. Place your desk so that you have a commanding view of the room. If you can't arrange your desk to face the door, try placing a small mirror on your desk or on the wall in front of you to provide a view of the doorway.

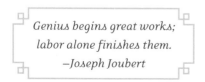

Genius begins great works;
labor alone finishes them.
—Joseph Joubert

KEYBOARD **CALM**

It is important to be aware of any tension in your hands, arms, shoulders, and neck as you tap the keys at your computer. Even if you maintain ideal posture while working, frequent breaks are essential to avoid aches in your upper body. Try this office Tai Chi technique to alleviate tightness and refresh yourself for the next task:

1 Sit comfortably in your chair.

2 Clasp your hands in front of you in a prayer position and breathe deeply.

3 Let your hands slowly sway like a cobra from side to side.

4 Feel the stretch in your wrists and forearms.

5 Move in slow motion as you calm down.

6 Next, interlace the fingers of both hands together in a tight fist.

7 Squeeze and massage both of your hands together and roll them in wide circles.

DRAWER **DRAGONS**

In the laws of feng shui: Out of sight is not out of mind.

The dragon is an ancient Chinese symbol for wealth and good fortune; stir the dragon's breath into your office drawers by keeping them in order. Hidden clutter blocks chi and is just as disabling as a mess on top of your desk. Organize things and you will feel more creative and less stressed. Plus, you will save time by not having to search for misplaced items. For those inevitable items that you don't immediately know what to do with, create a "procrastination drawer" for later consideration.

> *Real knowledge is to know the extent of one's ignorance.*
> *—Confucius*

Chapter Two
FENG SHUI FOR STRESS RELIEF
STAY CALM!

LESSONS IN **LETTING GO!**

To throw or not to throw—this is the question.

We all have a little bit of "pack rat" in us. Usually the excess stuff is rarely needed and simply takes up space. If you were guaranteed more success, energy, enthusiasm, and peace of mind in exchange for just a few minutes of clutter-clearing each day, you would most likely be open to it. Each time you bring your personal possessions into order, opportunity has more space to enter into your life. That's why people feel so much lighter when they let go of their stuff. It is also helpful to empty your wastebaskets daily to keep energy clear. Try letting go of the unnecessary clutter and notice the results in your well-being and success.

The goal of yesterday will be the starting point of tomorrow.
—Thomas Carlyle

AUSPICIOUS ATTITUDE

*Your attitude is the bridge that carries
your projects to completion!*

If you feel overwhelmed with negativity and torment, take
time to shift your mental state. Periodically repeating posi-
tive affirmations can get your thoughts back on track. Imag-
ine that you are your own inner coach. Don't be embarrassed
to cheer yourself on. Try repeating something like "Today I
will stay calm, confident, and caring in all my interactions."
Or, take a break and shift your body into motion. Getting your
blood pumping is also medicine for your mind. Go for a brisk
walk, ride a stationary bike, or take the stairs instead
of the elevator. Keep your personal feng
shui energy from stagnating by staying
physically and mentally active. If you
have been slaving away at your
desk, take a break and work out
both your mind and your body.

*He is able who
thinks he is able.*
–Buddha

COMMUNICATION CHI

*When having a discussion with a workmate
or client, remind yourself that communication
goes far beyond the words.*

Communication is a dance of chi between two or more people.
If one or all of you are frustrated, this will immediately stall
the exchange. Ask for feedback! Listen attentively and speak
slowly, clearly, and to the point. This will encourage under-
standing and create a supportive dialogue for everyone.

Rather than e-mailing your workmates, whenever possible
stir the chi in the office by going for a walk and delivering
messages to your colleagues in person. It's a nice break and
gives you a chance to get away from your desk. It also creates
a more intimate atmosphere among your coworkers, and
miscommunications are less likely to happen.

TEAMWORK **WISDOM**

A consciously arranged meeting space is key for a successful brainstorming session.

Auspicious meetings require preparation before people arrive. Create a Zen-like order with chairs evenly spaced, tables and blackboards clean, and all clutter and trash removed. Participants will feel the difference in the room and will produce better results. It's also helpful to play musical chairs after each break and have everyone sit in a different chair. Periodically shuffling the seating arrangement helps people stay focused and fresh. Always make sure participants have plenty of water to drink and are given breaks to maintain their focus.

If you are patient in one moment of anger, you will escape a hundred days of sorrow.
—Chinese proverb

INNER FENG SHUI

Stressful interactions and stressful surroundings can be transformed in seconds by simply taking a deep breath.

Deep breathing will help you open up for the next urgent project on your work agenda. For business success you must empty out your inner tension and create order and space within. It is the fastest route to balancing your inner feng shui.

- If you are feeling tense . . . take a deep, slow breath.

- If you are feeling sleepy . . . take a deep, powerful breath.

- The first step in every action is to take a deep breath for calmness and clarity.

- No matter what the situation . . . take a deep breath and then proceed!

> *Heroism consists of hanging on one minute longer.*
> *—Norwegian proverb*

YIN AND YANG SNACKS

Your body needs fuel to keep your internal chi flowing.

Eastern medicine classifies foods by their chi levels and their ability to influence your moods and creativity. Yang foods are warming and have an energizing effect, and yin foods are cooling for a calming effect. "Live" foods, such as fruits, vegetables, and nuts hold the highest level of chi and make for a good, quick snack. Avoid sugar-rich foods because they will inevitably make you sleepy and your thoughts unclear. Herbal tea, water, juice, and nuts are quick ways to help keep your chi in balance.

Eat regularly, choosing many snacks throughout the day rather than heavy meals. Yin foods include salads, fruits, and pasta. To maintain their yin quality, they should be raw or lightly cooked. Yang foods include meat, chicken, fish, roots, soups, and other foods that are better digested when cooked.

The quickest way to revitalize your inner chi is by drinking eight or more glasses of water throughout the day.

CUP OF **CHI!**

Sipping warm liquids soothes and calms the bodily systems.

Remember the three healthy Chinese G's: green tea, ginseng tea, and ginger tea. These teas tame your tension and keep you feeling healthy and energized throughout the day. Each has healing properties that assist in maintaining physical and mental health. When you need a boost, explore the benefits of these teas.

- **GREEN TEA** is a naturally stimulating source of antioxidants. It also helps you stay alert.

- **GINSENG TEA** has been celebrated for centuries to help boost your immune system against illness.

- **GINGER TEA** packs a punch and is a great choice when you are nursing a cold, as it will help clear your respiratory system.

MUSIC MAKEOVER

Office sounds often ignite tension and anxiety with
their constant ringing, clanging, and buzzing.

To help balance out the noise pollution, play some calming
music at a low volume to harmonize your work environment.
If music is not permissible, use a "white noise" producer,
such as a clock with a chime, a desktop fountain, or a fan. If
you have a CD player, natural sounds like ocean waves, falling
rain, a running stream, and blowing wind all are soothing.

> *We must either find*
> *a way or make one.*
> *–Hannibal*

EASY **ACUPRESSURE**

Just as chi flows like water through our outer environments, so it flows internally through our bodies.

When feeling stuck or stagnated, try stimulating these simple acupressure points to get your energy flowing again. These techniques will also help relieve everyday office stress and tension. Try these easy tips on both of your hands.

Mellow-Out Point.
Press your thumb into the middle of your palm. This spot is directly down from your middle and ring fingers. Take a few deep breaths and spend a moment relaxing the muscles in your body. Breathe and hold for a few moments.

Pain-in-the-Neck Pacifier.
Press one thumb into the soft tissue between your thumb and index finger. Relax your body and breathe calmly for a few moments. Firmly press on this point, letting your shoulders drop farther with each breath.

MIRROR MAGIC

> *It is helpful to use mirrors to direct chi to stagnant
> spaces, to reflect chi away from a place with too much
> energy, or to stop chi from rushing in a straight line.*

Mirrors can enhance the feeling of spaciousness and calm.
Place mirrors wherever you wish, but avoid hanging mirrors
facing each other, as the chi will bounce back and forth and
create a chaotic environment. Never hang a mirror directly
facing a door or a window, as the chi will empty out of the
room, and avoid mirrored tiles, as they fragment chi and
reflect it chaotically. When you mount a mirror, make sure
it is high enough on the wall that it won't cut off the top of
a person's head in their reflection.

BELLY OF THE DRAGON
IN THE OFFICE

Ancient feng shui philosophy states that the ideal place to live is in the Belly of the Dragon. This means a space where mountains support the back of the house and hills cradle the sides, while the front of the house faces the seashore. In the office, mountains and water can provide similar support.

Mountain of Support. Hanging a picture of mountains behind you provides a symbolic wall of support. You will feel more confident with the mountains backing you up. Avoid hanging images of hills, mountains, or big buildings directly facing toward you. These symbolize insurmountable challenges and obstacles that may block you and your projects.

Water Reflections. Water sets a soothing, reflective mood. We cannot always use real water in our offices, but adding a picture of water on your desk or a wall always works well. Scenes showing rivers, waterfalls, and lakes should always hang in front of you and never at your back. Having a picture of a water scene behind you can symbolize missed opportunity. When it is hanging in front of you or to your side, it is energizing and symbolic of abundance and health.

Chapter Three
FENG SHUI FOR PROSPERITY
BELIEVE IN YOUR SUCCESS!

POWER SPOT FOR PROSPERITY

When your work keeps you tied to your computer and you desperately need a break, take a desk retreat.

Make a clear space in the middle of your desk to help recapture your focus and calm. In the feng shui Desktop Map of Success (page 18) this area is the creative-power spot on your desk. Focus your eyes on this spot as you breathe gently in and out, feeling your body expand and contract. As you begin calming down, visualize success in your endeavors. When you feel that your confidence is restored, return to your projects, remembering that you are working in your creative-power spot for prosperity.

FENG SHUI YOUR WARDROBE

Dress for success!

Your personal chi expands outward from your body and impacts every interaction you have throughout the day. Choose colors to accent a particular mood you want to convey to those around you. According to feng shui philosophy, green exudes confidence, gray implies leadership, blue inspires creativity, yellow and brown provide a nurturing feeling, white radiates aliveness, red has a passionate impact, creamy colors exude a feeling of calm, and purple commands attention.

The next time you step into your closet, take notice of any excess. You most likely have favorite clothes alongside a large collection of rarely worn items. Some of your outfits may not represent who you are today. If you rarely wear an outfit, most likely it does not belong in your closet. Get rid of it.

GOOD FORTUNE 500

When you are busy and multitasking your way through the day, stress and a feeling of being overwhelmed can creep in.

That's the time to step away and sort through your office stuff. The moment you dig into your files and other possessions, you unlock your creativity. Keep moving your stuff around, organizing, cleaning, finding, throwing away, and refiling, until your mind is back in order. When you work from an empowered position, miracles can happen. Move your stuff five to five hundred times if necessary, until you are feeling like a Good Fortune 500 company.

Our greatest glory is not in never falling, but in rising every time we fall.
—Confucius

BALANCING YOUR **BILLS**

Disorganized bills can drain your finances and weigh heavily on your mind.

Make friends with your bills, treat them with respect, and place them in an orderly manner in a file folder or on a clipboard. Always be aware of what is due and when, and pay your bills on time. For credit cards and loans, make sure you are paying the lowest interest rates available. Not only is a good credit rating price-less but you want to stay in feng shui balance with your finances. Don't underestimate the small stuff in all areas of your life, including your money.

WISE WALLET
AND PURSE PLACEMENT

*Keep your purse and wallet in an
honorable place above the ground.*

To make positive changes in your finances, you must respect money—even your small change. Purchase a small, attractive change purse (black is a very auspicious color) and keep your coins stored in an orderly manner. Also be aware of how you store your folding money. If your bills are crumpled, loose, or otherwise in chaos, this also can show a lack of care for your finances. When your money details are in order, you will feel more at ease. Notice how the small actions you take with your money can blossom into a more powerful relationship with your finances.

> *Money is a good servant,
> but a bad master.*
> *—Henry Bohn*

LUCKY PENNIES

The Chinese invite prosperity by decorating a certain area of their home or office with three Chinese coins.

The number three invites good fortune, affixing coins onto a cash register, money box, or invoice book can increase your business luck. Or wrap three coins from any currency in red cloth and place them in an area through which you want the chi to flow more abundantly. Such actions will set you on a path to more prosperity. To energize important contracts or files, decorate their covers with coins or other auspicious symbols of wealth—such as a dollar bill, a picture of something elegant, or perhaps a photograph of a powerful nature scene.

When you are walking down the street and see a penny on the ground, pick it up—it may be your lucky penny.

PLANTS FOR
PROSPERITY

Where nature thrives, so do people.

Plants are one of the most common, practical, and attractive feng shui enrichments. Place greenery wherever you want to stimulate enthusiasm and abundance. Lucky bamboo, jade plants, and evergreens are some of the best flora for nourishing prosperity. It is important that you keep your plants watered and fresh. Dead plants in your office can create stagnation and bad luck; when fresh, they produce active, positive chi energy. Place a plant in an auspicious red pot to stimulate income. Or, display the plant in a section of the office that needs a dose of vitality.

> *You, yourself, as much as anybody in the universe, deserve your love and affection.*
> *—Buddha*

AQUARIUM **ASSET**

*Water in your personal office space will
bring excellent career luck.*

But don't overdo it—too much water in a small space can
drown your creativity! A small fountain is a wonderful desk-
top addition. It creates a soothing sound and is very calming
to gaze at. Most importantly, keep your fountain well main-
tained, with the water always filled and clean. You can also try
a small fishbowl to stimulate creativity. For a bigger effect,
such as to enhance company sales, install a large bubbling
aquarium in an appropriate area, such as the main foyer.
Shine bright lights directly into the aquarium and notice
how the aquarium can stimulate your company's business.

FENG SHUI **SHARING**

By bringing abundance and prosperity into other people's lives, you will see your own success flourish as well.

People blossom with nurturing gifts and kindness. Surprise a coworker with flowers! Or help someone organize and clean out a cluttered area in their office. It's fun to get into coworker's stuff and, side by side with them, organize their clutter. Sometimes people are so tied to their old possessions that it takes a gentle nudge from a friend to throw away unwanted baggage. Don't be surprised to see new opportunities arise from your generous efforts. Miraculous events have been known to occur when people "empty out the old and welcome in the new."

Chapter Four

FENG SHUI FOR THE ENTIRE OFFICE

CREATE NEW OPPORTUNITIES!

BETTER **BALANCE**

Yin and yang energies exist all around us. Yang is a more masculine, energetic, and dominating force. Yin is a more feminine, calming, subtle force.

Yang Office Energies. If you feel that your office is dull and stagnant, try introducing some more yang influence. Hang a nature painting on your wall or place an exciting postcard on your desk next to your computer. Play some passionate music or display a brightly colored cloth to stimulate this yang feeling.

Yin Office Energies. If you begin to feel exhausted and frustrated, spend some time putting your work away and clearing off your desk. Display items that help you feel calm and at peace, such as a small Buddha statue, and play some soft music or nature sounds.

MOUTH
OF CHI

*First impressions are very important. The front entry
of your company is a very auspicious area because it
is the main route for chi to flow into your building.*

When you arrive at work each day, use the main entrance, if
you can, for a confident entry. The foyer should be welcoming
and provide a buffer from the outside world. If you have a
foyer, keep this area well lit and open to invite good fortune
to your door. Keep unnecessary deliveries from piling up
here. It is important that the reception area be alive and the
air well circulated. Fans, plants, fountains, and other nature
features bring welcoming energy to the entrance. Mirrors
should be positioned to one side of the foyer so the chi will
not be reflected out the door. In Chinese philosophy, fish
tanks are considered the most auspicious feng shui addition to
the foyer. Fish symbolize wealth, prosperity, and good fortune.

OFFICE **BAGUA MAP**

*One of the most important tools in feng shui
philosophy is the bagua map.*

For centuries, feng shui practitioners have used the bagua
map to outline areas of a room that represent different aspects
of your life. The map divides space into nine compartments
to analyze the creative forces surrounding us. Simply look
around your office space and locate the different areas on
the map. To line up the Office Bagua Map correctly with your
office, align your front door with one of the bottom three map
areas, Wisdom, Career, or Contacts. On the following page
under "Office Bagua Enrichments," you will see a list of ideas
to enrich the nine different areas on the Office Bagua Map.

- The **PROSPERITY** area represents your wealth.

- The **FAME** area represents your relationship with the world.

- The **LOVE** area represents all of your relationships.

- The **CREATIVITY** area represents your ability to express yourself.

- The **CONTACTS** area represents the people who support you.

- The **CAREER** area represents your life purpose.

- The **WISDOM** area represents your knowledge of life.

- The **HEALTH** area represents the quality of life for you and your loved ones.

- The **BALANCE** area represents how you manage all the different aspects of your life.

BACK

prosperity	fame	love
health	balance	creativity
wisdom	career	contacts

LEFT SIDE

RIGHT SIDE

← DOORWAY →

OFFICE BAGUA **ENRICHMENTS**

*Study the Office Bagua Map on the previous page
and try some of the following enrichments.*

By making simple changes or additions to certain areas of
your space, you may be surprised by the profound changes
that will occur in your life. But don't be concerned if particu-
lar enrichment ideas don't fit into your office; just make the
changes that work for you.

- Light can make a bagua area feel clean and vibrant and
  bring life to hidden corners.

- Pleasant harmonies like music or nature sounds help calm
  bagua areas.

- Living objects such as a plant or flowers are great energy
  enhancers.

- Symbolic items, like a Buddha or religious icons, are
  inspirational and bring order to a bagua area.

- Moving objects, like water or chimes, make a bagua area feel
  more vibrant.

- Diplomas and certificates displayed on the desk or wall
  help build confidence in a certain bagua area.

- Colored cloth or pictures can add inspiration to a bagua area.

- Inspirational quotes and affirmations are a good way to
  enhance a bagua area.

Learning is a treasure that will follow its owner everywhere.
—Chinese proverb

CUBICLE **CHI**

Even though a cubicle is small and offers a limited barrier to the rest of the office, it still shelters you from the surrounding chaos.

Declare this area as your personal space, your home away from home. Add personal photos to make yourself feel comfortable. Hang small colorful pictures of nature and water to stimulate abundance and peace of mind. Displaying items that are small will make your cubicle appear much larger, which will help you feel less cramped.

CUBICLE **CURES**

By adding simple enrichments to your cubicle, you can create a more personal, comfortable, and empowered work space.

Welcome Mat. Set a small mat at your cubicle entrance. It will act as a buffer to the rest of the office. It will also encourage people to pause and announce themselves upon entering. When you limit the number of unannounced disturbances, your ability to focus will deepen.

Peeping Colleagues. It is helpful to place a tall plant at the entrance of your cubicle if there is a busy lane in front of your stall. This will provide a subtle distraction for those walking by, deterring colleagues from automatically focusing on you and your work.

Cubicle View. A small picture with a distant nature scene will make your cubicle seem larger. Gaze at the picture whenever you are feeling cramped in your space. It is important that you do not feel caged in your work space.

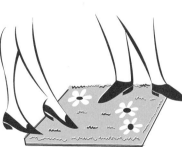

CLOSET CREATIVITY

*Closets, bookshelves, and cabinets are usually the
most neglected, disorganized areas in our work spaces.*

Since these locations are viewed by few, it's easy to let them
get out of control. In feng shui philosophy, each area of our
lives holds equal importance. Each box, file, or paper that we
possess is mentally stored away. To create more mental space,
it may be helpful to clear out and organize old stored items.

When possible, install doors on your shelves or cover them
with an attractive cloth. By making your files less visible, you
will improve the flow of chi and assist your efficiency and
relaxation. If a huge pile of
files is open to view, your
mind will be subconsciously
categorizing the items. Even
when your paperwork is out
of sight, it is still important
to organize your files. Out of
sight is not out of mind.

COLOR **YOUR WORLD**

Color is a powerful tool for changing the energy in your environment. To ignite good fortune, learn the ancient feng shui meanings behind specific colors.

GREEN is the color of plants and inspires growth in business; it has a calming, relaxing influence.

BLACK increases mental activity and improves communication. Black invites the mind to focus and contemplate decisions.

RED brings fame, good fortune, and happiness when properly used. Many feng shui enrichments employ red envelopes, red ink for calligraphy, and red ribbons. Red dispels bad luck and attracts positive energy.

WHITE encourages prosperity and abundance and has a very calming effect in an office. It increases determination, mental clarity, and sharp focus.

YELLOW and **BROWN** are earthy colors. They symbolize stability in your life and help you stay grounded. Yellow is representative of the sun and its nourishing warmth and promotes feelings of optimism and cheerfulness.

Feel free to use these colors when adding feng shui enrichments into your office space. Check the Office Bagua Map (page 65) and the Desktop Map of Success (page 18) for ideas on where in your office you can place these colors for inspiration.

ELECTRIC ENERGY

*All electrical equipment and appliances generate
electromagnetic fields, known as EMFs.*

Exposure to EMFs and dissonant noises can drain your
energy, interfere with your concentration, and generally
make you irritable. Do some research about purchasing a
negative-ion generator to counteract office air pollution.
When you take a break, go for a walk and separate yourself
from copiers, faxes, printers, computers, and other electrical
equipment. It is helpful to place a live plant beside you or
between you and your electrical equipment to help clear the
air, dampen noise, and energize your chi. Since most every-
day business noises tend to grate on your nerves over time,
when possible turn off equipment that is not being used.

LIGHT UP
YOUR LIFE

*Fluorescent lights generally
leave you feeling tired and grumpy.*

If you have a say in the type of lighting in your office, ask for
full-spectrum lighting. If it's impossible to alter the general
lighting in your office, set up your own desk lamp with the
incandescent bulb of your choice. This will create a pool of
gentle light on your work area that causes less eyestrain and
helps you concentrate. Place the lamp on your desk on the
opposite side from your dominant hand, so that you don't cast
shadows on your work. An adjustable lamp can pour light
into dark corners where chi may be stagnating. Try to block
the glare on your computer screen, since glare is an eyesore.
According to feng shui philosophy, glare reflects positive
chi away from you. Well-balanced lighting can also alleviate
headaches, squinting, and eyestrain.

> *Success is getting what you want;
> happiness is wanting what you get.*
> —Dale Carnegie

HOME WORK

Business Hours. If you work at home, set business hours for yourself and stick to them. It doesn't matter when in the day you work, as long as you follow your work hours. This way you're less apt to slip into your office during off hours. Your children will respect your privacy more if they know your work hours. You can even post them on the door.

Do Not Disturb. When you are working in your home office, try to keep interruptions to a minimum. Create a "Do Not Disturb" sign and place it visibly on the entrance to your office. You will ensure peace and quiet and will be able to fully focus on your business.

Bells to Boost Business. Feng shui philosophy says that hanging bells on your office door handle can increase business. A small bell that sounds whenever someone enters can help trigger your mind to switch into business gear.

> *Do not dwell in the past, do not dream of the future, concentrate the mind on the present moment.*
> *—Buddha*

Chapter Five
FENG SHUI ON THE GO
PROMOTE YOUR DREAMS!

CHI **FLOW**

*Chi flows through our environment like
invisible rivers and streams.*

Go for a walk in your office and see if you can feel the
currents of chi flowing through it. Some of your work
areas will feel comfortable, clean, and in order, while
others won't—here the chi is stuck in chaos and clutter.
This unhealthy chi can create bad luck, ill health, and
a feeling of frustration. Develop an eye for where bad
chi accumulates like a spider's web. For example: dark
corners, awkward furniture arrangements, piles of
stuff, and dirty surfaces. Once you can recognize where
chi may be stuck, you can apply some easy feng shui
enrichments, such as those suggested in the Desktop
Map of Success (page 18) and the Office Bagua Map
(page 65). Some helpful enrichments include electric
fans, bright lights, open spaces, conscious placement
of furniture, beautiful plants, and ornaments.

*I'm a great believer in luck, and I find
the harder I work, the more I have of it.*
—Thomas Jefferson

YIN AND YANG
ON THE GO

As you make your way through your day on errands and appointments, try to maintain peace of mind. While you're on the go, it helps to take a rejuvenating break.

To Calm. Nourish your yin energy by sitting quietly for a while. Drink some soothing tea. Manage your energy, and focus on returning to a calm state. Take a few deep breaths and let your body relax. Drop your shoulders and slow the many thoughts running through your mind.

To Energize. Energize your yang energy by walking briskly and waking up your sluggish body. Stand straight and feel your body rise upward. Take full, deep breaths and notice your mind becoming more alert with each exhalation. When you pump up your enthusiasm, you will be less likely to struggle through your errands.

There are no traffic jams when you go the extra mile.
—Anonymous

CELL-PHONE **SERENITY**

Your cell phone is an integral part of your business—especially when you're on the go.

It's essential to use a cell phone that fits comfortably in your hand, has a long battery life, and works with a wireless headset or has a speakerphone so you can avoid neck strain. While out and about, try to make your calls without distractions. Cell phones are an ultimate test in calm, since calls often come at the most inopportune times. Most importantly, try not to disturb others. Feng shui harmony affects every area of your life and all of those with whom you interact. While you are traveling you may want to designate times when your cell phone is off, so you can take an undisturbed break.

FENG SHUI YOUR **BRIEFCASE**

When you are on the go, your briefcase is an extension of you and your office.

If you are buying a new briefcase, black is an auspicious feng shui color, as it represents income and money. When black is combined with metal, the feng shui symbolism is even more auspicious—so look for one with metallic clasps.

Make sure you are well equipped for your meetings, and have your briefcase fully stocked with extra cell-phone batteries, a snack, and water. Put your portable office in order and make it inspiring for your work. Empty out old material that is not needed. An overstuffed briefcase blocks healthy chi and will spill over into your other business. On the inside of your briefcase you can tape a picture of loved ones or an inspiring message for reassurance on the road.

A happy heart is better than a full purse.
—Italian proverb

ORGANIZED INNER ITINERARY

Travel can be chaotic and nerve-racking.

To ensure a pleasant trip, follow this travel preparation plan:

1   Make sure your travel documents and ID are easily accessible for quick use.

2   Have all required names, addresses, and phone numbers prepared beforehand.

3   Make sure all details regarding accommodations have been researched and booked.

4   What special needs do you have? Perhaps you should bring along the name of a good massage therapist or the address of a gym or yoga studio.

5   Have a change purse with coins and small bills handy for tipping porters and other travel expenses.

By being prepared, you'll limit distractions and arrive at your destination with your peace of mind intact.

A wise man will make more opportunities than he finds.
—Francis Bacon

CAR CONSCIOUSNESS

*Imagine the time you spend in your car
as an opportunity to calm down.*

If you arrive at work or meetings feeling stressed and
frazzled, your performance will obviously suffer. Since your
car often becomes a mobile office, it is handy to stock some
business supplies there. Also keep a stash of nourishing
snacks and drinks for the road. Have a selection of music
to match your desired mood. Bring an overnight bag just in
case you need to do a midday clothes switch. By keeping the
interior and exterior of your vehicle clean, you will feel nice
and refreshed at the end of your journey.

ENLIGHTENED ENTERTAINING

*For a lunch meeting, situate yourself in
a power spot where you can see the front
door and have your back to a wall.*

When you arrive at the restaurant, make a mental note of the
room arrangement. Stay away from heavily trafficked areas,
especially the kitchen door. This will eliminate surprises and
leave you feeling more at ease. If possible, arrive early and
introduce yourself to the maitre d' or manager. Let them
know how important it is for you and your clients to feel at
home. You want to be comfortable and empowered.

*I hear and I forget.
I see and I remember.
I do and I understand.
—Confucius*

HOTEL-ROOM RESUSCITATION

When traveling, it's a good idea to bring along some personal items that make you feel at home in your hotel room.

Trust your intuition and spend time contemplating how you can transform your new living quarters for utmost feng shui good fortune and comfort. Candles and incense can help cleanse the room of the prior occupants' energy and help you feel relaxed in your surroundings. Keep the bathroom door closed to stop opportunity from flowing down the toilet. Don't be afraid to move the furniture around for your comfort and good fortune. Position your work space toward the door, if possible. Bring your own soothing music to play; nothing can make you feel at ease more than your favorite songs. An attractive cloth placed on one of the tables creates an altar for flowers, personal items, and photos of loved ones. As a way of giving and devotion, before checking out, leave your room neat in order to assist the maid.

MESMERIZING **MEISHI**

Make your business cards very auspicious!

In Japan, the *meishi* (business card) is considered an extremely important symbol for yourself and your company. A company logo carries powerful chi. If you can design your own card, pay careful attention to how it looks. The layout and logo should incorporate good-fortune symbols. In China, the dragon is one of the luckiest symbols. Choose a symbol that is powerful, friendly, and exudes a feeling of success and prosperity. Logos are felt before they are thought about, and the picture will linger in people's minds. If the message is carried across successfully, people will consider your business to be professional and trustworthy. Offer your card with enthusiasm and goodwill.

FLYING FENG SHUI

Navigating through an airport often leaves people feeling ragged.

This does not need to be your reality. Arrive early and make maintaining a calm state of mind your priority. While waiting to check in for your flight, put your bags down and assume the preparatory Tai Chi stance: Stand with both feet firmly planted on the ground and your weight evenly distributed. Relax your body and mind, and note if your shoulders or other areas of your body are tense.

When holding your bags, try to keep the weight evenly distributed. Bend your knees slightly, with your posture straight and your chest out. Keep bringing your mind back to the present moment and patiently wait for your turn. Take a deep relaxing breath each time you become restless and impatient. Look at lines as unplanned breaks; you can use this time to review your schedule. Once you master the art of waiting, you will look forward to your airport retreats.

What you do not wish upon yourself, extend not to others.
—Confucius

AIRPLANE **TAI CHI**

These Tai Chi exercises will help you get more comfortable and cozy for your flight. When you spend a little time doing these in-flight exercises, you'll feel fewer aches and pains upon arrival.

Energized Entertainment. While airborne and in your seat, twist your feet in wide circles, one foot at a time. Feel the chi energy rising from your feet up into the rest of your body. This Tai Chi move will help ease your fears and settle you down. Remember to relax and breathe as you stretch.

Seated Swim. To help relieve neck and shoulder tightness from carrying heavy bags, try stretching your shoulders in wide circles in a swimming motion, one at a time. Move slowly, relax, and breathe, feeling relief in your upper body. Now reverse the circles.

> *Teachers open the door,*
> *but you must enter by yourself.*
> *—Chinese proverb*

BIOGRAPHIES

Photo by Rebecca Lawson

Darrin Zeer, a relaxation consultant for corporations, is the best-selling author of *Office Yoga, Office Spa,* and *Everyday Calm,* all available from Chronicle Books. He travels around North America encouraging people to stay calm, enjoy their work, and be successful. He has appeared on CNN, in *The Wall Street Journal* and *Time* magazine, on NPR radio and Web MD, and in hundreds of other media venues. Darrin spent seven years in Asia studying the Eastern arts of yoga and meditation. He lives in California, where he writes and consults for companies like 3M, Four Seasons Hotels and Resorts, CNN, and the Food Bank.

If you would like Darrin to work with your company, visit him on the Web at www.relaxationconsultants.com.

Frank Montagna is a Los Angeles-based freelance illustrator whose work includes *Office Spa*. His illustrations appear in a variety of publications, including *New York* magazine, *The Wall Street Journal, Cosmo Girl!, Modern Bride*, and *Glamour* (Germany). He also works in television as a production and character designer, and has done animation work for Walt Disney Feature Animation and MTV.

ACKNOWLEDGMENTS

Special thanks to my editor, Jodi Davis, and the rest of the team at Chronicle Books. Thank you to John Mapleback, John Pine, and Dawn Wilson for their editing assistance and moral support. Thanks to my parents, Carole and Louis Zeer, and also Monique, Rob, Michelle, Cindy, Cynthia, Damien, Abheeru, Dustin, Marcus, Kris, Christoph, Dave, Siegmar, Catherine, Hans, Blaze, Ginny, and G'Angela.

Learn to live in a place of love.
—Kalindi la Gourasana

ENJOY **"DOUBLE HAPPINESS"**
ON THE JOB . . .

peace and enjoyment
with unlimited success!